Designs for Glass Etching
49 Full-Size Motifs

by Robert G. Bush

Dover Publications, Inc., New York

 Publisher's Note

IN RECENT YEARS, the art of etching glass, so popular in the final quarter of the nineteenth century and the first quarter of the twentieth, has enjoyed a new popularity. Consequently, craftspeople find themselves in need of new patterns. This book supplies 49 motifs, reproduced full-size, which include florals, animals, fish and birds. In many instances, corner elements are supplied, as well as reduced illustrations showing possible ways in which the motifs can be assembled for a project. Page 46 is devoted entirely to such suggestions.

The reader who is interested in instructions on the craft of etching glass, as well as additional patterns and numerous hints on adapting and combining pattern elements, is referred to *Glass Etching: 46 Full-Size Patterns with Complete Instructions* by Robert A. Capp and Robert G. Bush (Dover, ISBN 0-486-24578-0).

Copyright © 1989 by Robert G. Bush.
All rights reserved under Pan American and International Copyright Conventions.

Published in Canada by General Publishing Company, Ltd., 30 Lesmill Road, Don Mills, Toronto, Ontario.
Published in the United Kingdom by Constable and Company, Ltd.

Designs for Glass Etching: 49 Full-Size Motifs is a new work, first published by Dover Publications, Inc., in 1989.

Manufactured in the United States of America
Dover Publications, Inc., 31 East 2nd Street, Mineola, N.Y. 11501

Library of Congress Cataloging-in-Publication Data

Bush, Robert G.
  Designs for glass etching : 49 full-size motifs / by Robert G. Bush.
      p.   cm.
  ISBN 0-486-26000-3
  1. Glass etching—Themes, motives. I. Title.
NK5201.B87   1989
748.6—dc19   89-30383
                                                        CIP

4

Application shown on page 46.

23

Application shown on page 46.

45

(p. 19)

(p. 32)

(p. 29)

Full-size motifs are to be found on the pages indicated.